REVIVING OUR INTRINSIC SENSE

Changing the World One "Peace" at a Time

JILL HOUSTON

Reviving Our Intrinsic Sense
Copyright © 2020 by Jill Houston

All rights reserved. No part of this publication may be reproduced, distributed, or transmitted in any form or by any means, including photocopying, recording, or other electronic or mechanical methods, without the prior written permission of the author, except in the case of brief quotations embodied in critical reviews and certain other non-commercial uses permitted by copyright law.

Tellwell Talent
www.tellwell.ca

ISBN
978-0-2288-3816-6 (Hardcover)
978-0-2288-3815-9 (Paperback)
978-0-2288-3817-3 (eBook)

The commonly known senses:

Touch, sight, hearing, smell, and taste

The yet to be revived sense:

Intrinsic: Belonging to the essential nature or constitution of a thing

This is for all the people who would like to feel peace but cannot invest the time in understanding why they are unable to achieve it. For many it may also highlight that they truly are not peaceful and not even cognizant of it.

Part 1

Me

Reviving Our Intrinsic Sense

First, I am not a doctor, nor am I highly religious or formally educated on the topic of intrinsic sense; however, I have done a lot of reading and practising based on it and feel a wider acceptance would be achieved if it were simplified.

For the better part of 2019 I watched as my mother chose to die. She refused treatments, lived with agonizing pain, and finally died on her birthday, July 21st, 2019. At her funeral I was standing with my Dad beside her casket and his words really struck me. First, he said how she looked 20 years younger, and then stated neither he nor my mom were afraid to die—it was the getting there that was hard. She did it her way.

Within a few months of my moms passing, my relationship ended, my dog died, and my father was diagnosed with advanced cancer and dementia. I left my job, re-located back to my hometown, and decided to dedicate 50% of my time to helping my sister and her partner care for my father. My father is a retired United Church minister who had spent 30-plus years helping others cope with their grief. However, I soon learned that he really did not know how to deal with his own, opting for keeping busy to avoid feeling. I also recognized that the people of this world, myself included, were not good at feeling or understanding what feeling really meant.

I had spent many years practising yoga and mindfulness. Both were great at controlling my current moment, but neither addressed all the past moments and how they played out in my everyday life. Could mindfulness become a non-event if I were able to address the intrinsic emotions that required me to execute mindfulness in the first place? Could addressing these intrinsic emotions allow my mind to live mindfully automatically?

And so the journey began in January 2020. The canvas I had to work with was defined by being a smoker, moderately poor eater, drinker, medicated depressive, and intimate-relationship challenged partner. As much as this seems like a long list, I could have also been defined as being active, loved by family and friends, compassionate, and career successful. Could I, through healing my intrinsic self, enable my poor habits to dissolve naturally and mindfulness to become a way of life?

This is when I was introduced to Michael Brown and *The Presence Process*. His book introduced me to the art of realizing that my repressed internal energy was the causal point of my unrest. The Universe is comprised of 100% energy, and this includes all its contents, including me. In 1845 James Prescott Joule discovered the first law of thermodynamics: **Energy cannot be created or destroyed.**

Having studied all this material I, of course, wanted my friends and family to follow suit. I shared articles, books and dialogue but soon realized that the content was, in many cases, too overwhelming, and therefore few took part… This was the impetus for me writing this succinct narrative. I have found that the things I have learned were of such great value that maybe, just maybe, if I could make the message simpler then more people would understand and we, as a society, could start to change our direction to be something more respectful of the human race and our Universe. If we feel peace, we project peace, and when enough of us are doing that the hostilities of the world become more peaceful.

Please note that this narrative will not explain the "why" as has been so beautifully captured by many before me. It will, however, directly explain the "how" through which it can be achieved in a user-friendly fashion that has had a profound impact on my life.

Part 2

Intrinsic Sense

Reviving Our Intrinsic Sense

Have you ever awoken and not felt quite right? Have you ever been with a family member and felt on guard? Have you ever been in a relationship and wondered why you are not getting along? Have you ever felt anxious about something for no known reason? Do you feel the constant need to be doing things or to be with people? All these sensations are being governed by your intrinsic sense.

In its purest form, our intrinsic sense reflects the genetics we have been handed from previous generations along with the emotions we learned throughout our first 7 years of life. Unfortunately, through generations of scars and masking, along with our own early life experiences, this pure form becomes distorted. This internal energy remains as such until we learn to dissipate the distortions. This energy is what causes our everyday-life reactions and because it is masked and scarred, inhibits us, in many circumstances, from living in a peaceful way. We avoid this energy blockage through changing our companions, altering our physical circumstances, and using suppressants such as smoking, drinking, drugging, or poor eating. We do this because we are no longer in tune with our physiological feelings, because it is easier to run away than try to heal them.

Law of attraction: **The belief that the universe creates and provides for you that which your thoughts are focused on.**

Law of cause and effect: **Every effect has a specific and predictable cause. Every cause or action has a specific and predictable effect. This means that everything that we currently have in our lives is an effect that is a result of a specific cause.**

The question is, how can you change the cause and therefore alter the effect?

First, accept that you have this underlying intrinsic sense that we all have ignored for millennia. Whenever you feel unrest this sense is active. Whenever you feel good this sense is active. Triggers to this sense come from input from your other senses, even through something like waking from a bad dream. All will cause some sort of physiological sensation. This is what needs to be healed.

When we live in this state we attract based on our scarred and masked energy. When we live in this state, what we do produces effects based on our scarred and masked energy. What we need to do is heal this energy to attract based on our pure self. When we attract based on our pure self, we will produce unscarred and unmasked effects.

How:

Step 1: Physiologically feel the sense and do not try to change it—just recognize it and be with it. I do this by closing my eyes, keeping my mind clear, and

Reviving Our Intrinsic Sense

sitting quietly with my body. Once attuned, you will start to sense the energy running within you. Your heart centre (solar plexus) may have an ache, your shoulders may be sore, your arms or legs may tingle. Whatever the sensation, be with it and stay with it until it dissipates…and it will…but because we have been in the ignore mode for so long this practise will take time.

Step 2: Do this daily at a specific time, as well as whenever the unrest exists. Take time to be with it, as it holds the key to you changing how your thoughts are manifested and how you act. Once this new sense is brought into your daily life, peace will start to appear more frequently.

Step 3: Start to notice over time how your life starts to incrementally change. Take time to sense not only the unrest but also the calmness. Notice how your interactions with others are calmer and how you start to respond to challenges instead of reacting to them. This calmness represents peace.

The first time you can feel the sensation dissipate is magical. I achieved this some 6 months ago and continue to practise daily. It will take time, but it must be part of your everyday routine.

René Descartes wrote: "I think, therefore I am"

… Should this not be: 'I am and, therefore, I think?'

Part 3

Intrinsic Sense and Mindfulness

Mindfulness: **Mindfulness is the psychological process of purposely bringing one's attention to experiences occurring in the present moment without judgment.**

If we become masters at revising and healing our intrinsic sense, our minds will ultimately exist in the present moment. Even though this is still a work in progress for me, I have had enough experiences to show it as a truth. Until complete intrinsic sensing is achieved, mindfulness remains an important tool. The challenge with mindfulness is that it addresses the wandering mind but does not ever heal the internal energy, therefore it is a mask…an important mask, but nonetheless a mask.

Part 4

Intrinsic Sense and Intimate Relationships

Opposites do not attract. Our emitted energy attracts, and because our energy is scarred and masked, the person we attract reflects that which we need to heal in ourselves. Without addressing our energy, we will be destined to continue to repeat this cycle. Once we have healed our scars and removed our masks, the person we attract will be based on a pure version of ourselves.

<u>My personal example</u>

A world governed by a mask and scarred intrinsic sense:

I have lived my life based on my masked and scarred intrinsic sense. Until recently, I spent much of this time in a relationship that lasted eight years.

At first there was love and I had no idea I had set myself up with someone who would reflect my masked and scarred intrinsic sense. At the time I was not aware of this underlying energy, nor did I have the skills to heal it. Countless couples' therapy sessions hinted at this, but none came right out and said what was going on and what I had to do. Note, the greater the attraction, the more likely the person will be to trigger your adverse energy. Only after the end of the relationship, and through many exercises in allowing my energy to dissipate, did I come to realize that what I was experiencing had nothing to do with the other individual but had everything to do with the need for me to heal. This has been a life-changing gift to me.

How my masked and scarred intrinsic sense manifested itself time and time again:

A word would be said, or an event would take place and I would react. My reaction would be based on the scars and masks I have within. These represented my triggers and buttons and therefore my masks and scars which my internal energy would be holding… Absolutely nothing to do with the person or event would be the real cause. This reaction would cause an equal and opposite reaction which ultimately apexed into a fight and a greater distance between us. We did not know how to release our own energy or help the other release theirs. After enough time the relationship ended. I then vowed never to be in another relationship or, if I were to be in another relationship and not want to have the same outcome, I would need to better understand my own energy.

How this would have unfolded with a purified unmasked and unscarred intrinsic sense:

First, one or both parties must have done work on themselves. Ideally both would have done the work but one partner who is in tune with his or her intrinsic sense can help guide the other.

In the above case, had I been more attuned, I would have acknowledged that my partner was not the cause of my unrest nor my reactions. I would have recognized this and used my internal tools to acknowledge my energy and allow it to dissipate. This does not mean the event would not have required a response. The new response would have been one without masks or scars and would have represented how I innately felt.

In the event my partner were not in tune with their own energy and did react (rather than respond), my role would have been to acknowledge that I am not the source of their reaction and provide comfort to them in their state of unrest. This comfort, without defensiveness, would also allow the dissipation of their scars/masks to take place, allowing for further communication if required.

If we feel peace, we project peace, and when enough of us are doing that the hostilities of the world become more peaceful.

Intrinsic sense and parenting:

I do not have kids but am blessed with having many families as part of my inner circle. The things I have learned from acknowledging energy is also truly relevant to the family unit. The thing that frustrates you most with your kids represents an energy within yourself that needs to be released. They are being your trigger as you are being theirs. The same process as described earlier should be used for this to be addressed in a mature fashion. The parent should take the lead. When frustrated, look within, allow the energy to dissipate, and then respond in a pure way. The fact that the parent can teach this to the child could be life changing.

Part 5

Intrinsic Sense and World Peace

Reviving Our Intrinsic Sense

The world is in a crazy place. Leaders of all types have attempted to make our existence peaceful with extraordinarily little success. I believe world peace must come from the individual, and when critical mass is achieved the world landscape will start to shift to a more peaceful existence. This can only be done when we find peace within ourselves.

If we feel peace, we project peace, and when enough of us are doing that, the hostilities of the world become more peaceful.

My landscape update: I am still on my journey, have weened myself off of the anti-depressants, and have noticed a considerable reduction in all of the self-destructive behaviours, behaviours I believe will end one day…when it is time…and when I have healed. Please note that this is not because I have put myself through some huge quitting drama counting the days until I am complete. It is because I have evolved, I am healing, and I no longer feel the need.

JCH

www.ingramcontent.com/pod-product-compliance
Lightning Source LLC
LaVergne TN
LVHW042005060526
838200LV00041B/1884